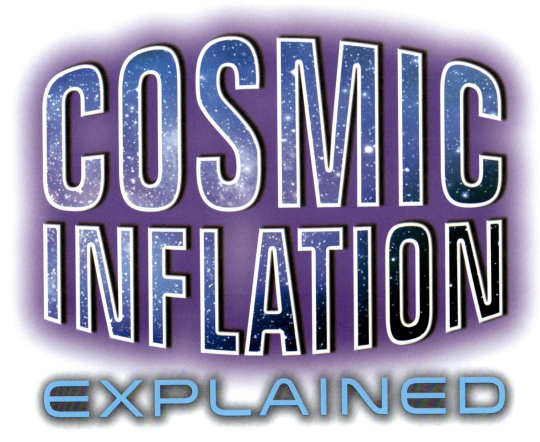

THE MYSTERIES OF SPACE

COSMIC INFLATION

EXPLAINED

KELLY BLUMENTHAL

Enslow Publishing
101 W. 23rd Street
Suite 240
New York, NY 10011
USA

enslow.com

Published in 2019 by Enslow Publishing, LLC.
101 W. 23rd Street, Suite 240, New York, NY 10011

Copyright © 2019 by Enslow Publishing, LLC.

All rights reserved.

No part of this book may be reproduced by any means without the written permission of the publisher.

Library of Congress Cataloging-in-Publication Data

Names: Blumenthal, Kelly, author.
Title: Cosmic inflation explained / Kelly Blumenthal.
Description: New York, NY : Enslow Publishing, [2019] | Series: The mysteries of space | Audience: Grades 7 to 12. | Includes bibliographical references and index.
Identifiers: LCCN 2017054728| ISBN 9780766099531 (library bound) | ISBN 9780766099548 (pbk.)
Subjects: LCSH: Inflationary universe—Juvenile literature. | Expanding universe—Juvenile literature. | Cosmology—Juvenile literature. | Hubble, Edwin, 1889-1953—Juvenile literature.
Classification: LCC QB991.I54 B58 2018 | DDC 523.1/8—dc23
LC record available at https://lccn.loc.gov/2017054728

Printed in the United States of America

To Our Readers: We have done our best to make sure all website addresses in this book were active and appropriate when we went to press. However, the author and the publisher have no control over and assume no liability for the material available on those websites or on any websites they may link to. Any comments or suggestions can be sent by email to customerservice@enslow.com.

Photos Credits: Cover Andrea Danti/Shutterstock.com; p. 5 d1sk/Shutterstock.com; p. 7 Anadolu Agency/Getty Images; p. 11 Peter Hermes Furian/Shutterstock.com; pp. 12, 14, 22, 24 (graph), 36, 51 Kelly Blumenthal; pp. 16, 45, 64, 65 Designua /Shutterstock.com; p. 17 AVKost/Shutterstock.com; p. 18 NOAO/AURA/NSF /Science Source; p. 24 (Dr. Rubin) The Washington Post/Getty Images; p. 25 NC Collections/Alamy Stock Photo; p. 28 koya979/Shutterstock.com; p. 32 Jon Brenneis/The LIFE Images Collection/Getty Images; p. 33 David A. Hardy /Science Source; p. 38 Frank Whitney/The Image Bank/Getty Images; p. 41 (top, left) Print Collector/Hulton Archive/Getty Images; p. 41 (top, right) SSPL/Getty Images; p. 41 (bottom) NASA 382199/Corbis News/Getty Images; p. 43 Ted Thai/The LIFE Picture Collection/Getty Images; p. 48 Mark Garlick/Science Source; p. 49 snapgalleria/Shutterstock.com; p. 58 Rhys Taylor/Stocktrek Images/Getty Images; p. 60 Universal History Archive/Universal Images Group/Getty Images; p. 67 Getty Images; back cover and interior pages sdecoret/Shutterstock.com (earth's atmosphere from space), clearviewstock/Shutterstock.com (space and stars).

CONTENTS

Introduction
6

Chapter One
The 5 Percent: How Do We See the Universe?
9

Chapter Two
The Other 95 Percent: Dark Matter and Dark Energy
20

Chapter Three
Hubble's Legacy
31

Chapter Four
The Far Reaches of the Observable Universe
39

Chapter Five
Cosmic Inflation: Something from Nothing
46

Chapter Six
The Past, Present, and Future of Our Universe
55

Chapter Seven
Unanswered Questions in Cosmology
62

Chapter Notes 69
Glossary 73
Further Reading 76
Index 78

INTRODUCTION

All of humanity exists on a single planet, Earth, in a system that orbits an unimpressive star, the sun. The solar system is one of thousands in our Milky Way alone, and our galaxy is one of billions. Our universe is incredibly vast, and understanding it (and our place within it) is perhaps the most human endeavor.

Mankind has attempted to understand the universe for thousands of years, and the definition is constantly changing. From about 5000 BCE, ancient Egyptians carefully studied the motions of the stars in the night sky. Many of their structures were built to be aligned with the stars or the direction of the setting or rising sun on the solstices. By the time the pyramids at Giza were built, the standard 365-day calendar was already in use. To the ancient Greeks, astronomy was a way to mathematically determine the motions of the heavens. Many of these early astronomers were also philosophers, mathematicians, artists, and musicians. It was thought that there was a deep connection between these practices: one that could be revealed through numbers. Polynesians and the first Hawaiians used astronomy, oceanography, and meteorology to navigate the vast Pacific Ocean. All of these cultures (and multitudes more around the globe) sought to understand and define the world as they experienced it. With the advent of calculus in the seventeenth century, there was finally a rigorous mathematical language to

INTRODUCTION

Twice a year in Aswan, Egypt, the statues at the Abu Simbel temple are illuminated by the rising sun. Archaeologists believe that monuments such as these were built to mark the start (and end) of the agricultural season.

talk about the world around us. Physicists and astronomers such as Cecilia Payne, Albert Einstein, Subrahmanyan Chandrasekhar, Emmy Noether, Stephen Hawking, Vera Rubin, and many others have built off of the discoveries made over thousands of years.

7

COSMIC INFLATION EXPLAINED

One such scientist, Alan Guth (1947–), an MIT physicist, developed the theory of cosmic inflation. Imagine that everything you know exists on the surface of a balloon. Imagine next that the balloon is expanding faster than you can see with your eyes, to something far larger than we can observe. This is analogous to cosmic inflation. Cosmic inflation is the process by which our universe got to be the way it is today. Guth first came up with the theory of cosmic inflation in the 1970s to help alleviate some of the major inconsistencies in the big bang theory. Since then, cosmic inflation and the big bang theory have become the prevailing theories for how our universe began.

Chapter One

The 5 Percent: How Do We See the Universe?

According to the best theories astronomers and physicists could come up with, the universe started with a bang. The big bang theory states that the universe originated from an infinitely hot, infinitely dense, and infinitely small point, called a singularity. Everything in the universe known today came from that single point. The first step to understanding how the universe got to be the size it is today is to understand what it's made of and how it is observed.

Imagine everything in your house, all the houses on your block, all the blocks in your town. Think about Earth and the solar system. All the stars in the sky. Our galaxy. All of the galaxies in the universe. All of that only comprises roughly 5 percent of the stuff in the universe.[1] This is ordinary matter. Everything people can touch, smell, see, and interact with makes up the tiniest fraction of the universe.

The Electromagnetic Spectrum

Almost everything in the universe that people are familiar with—stars and galaxies and objects between—emits some kind of light. Light is organized on the electromagnetic spectrum. One can think of light in terms of its wavelength or its energy. Low energy light has a long wavelength, while high energy light has a very short wavelength. From high to low energy, there is gamma ray, X-ray, ultraviolet, visible, infrared, microwave, and radio.

Some of these types of light are used in everyday appliances. Radios use light waves to transmit sound. A microwave uses microwaves to heat up food. Someone who uses night goggles can see the world around them in the infrared (basically just heat). The visible spectrum—what can actually be seen with the eyes—is a very small fraction of the electromagnetic spectrum. The ultraviolet rays from the sun are why it is necessary to wear and reapply sunscreen when outside. Someone with a broken bone may get an X-ray. Gamma rays have so much energy, they're used on Earth to fight cancer. Out in the cosmos, they're fairly rare; only the most energetic phenomena in the universe produce gamma rays.

Blackbody Radiation

One way to increase the energy of an object is to heat it up. Everything in the universe (if it has some kind of heating source,

THE 5 PERCENT: HOW DO WE SEE THE UNIVERSE?

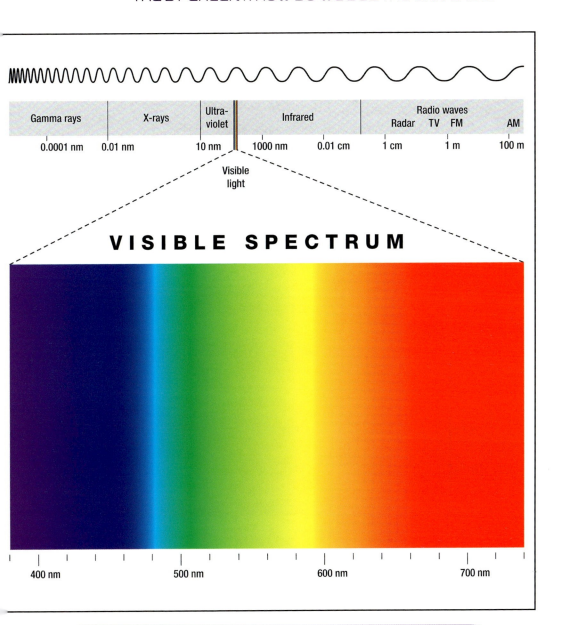

Light is organized on the electromagnetic (EM) spectrum. The part of the EM spectrum that we can see with our eyes is known as the visible spectrum. This is only a tiny fraction of all possible kinds of light. Low energy light has a long wavelength, while high energy light has a very short wavelength.

COSMIC INFLATION EXPLAINED

such as a stove, a beating heart, or nuclear fusion) emits thermal radiation, or heat. In physics and astronomy, temperatures are typically given in units of Kelvin (K). There isn't a degree symbol. This is because Kelvin is a true unit of temperature, based on "absolute zero," while Fahrenheit and Centigrade are gradations of temperature based on the boiling and freezing points of water. Typically, hot, radiating objects don't just emit light at

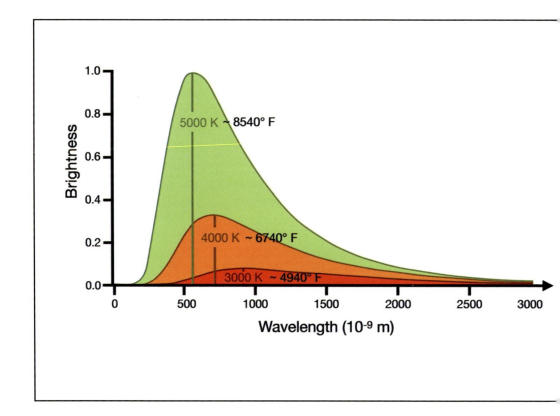

This graph shows examples of blackbody radiation of objects at different temperatures. The area under the green curve is larger than the area under the orange or red curves, indicating that objects at higher temperatures are brighter.

one wavelength; there is some amount of light emitted at all wavelengths. If one could measure how much light is emitted at each wavelength (the brightness) due to an object's heating source, it would have a very specific shape that is dependent only on its temperature. This is known as blackbody radiation. The color observed depends on the object's temperature.

Hotter objects not only emit more light, but they have a peak in their brightness at a shorter wavelength (i.e. higher energy). If two objects have the same temperature, they will produce the same blackbody radiation curve. For example, a regular incandescent light bulb heats up to about 11,000°F (6,093°C). That's approximately the temperature of the surface of the sun. Were one to compare their respective brightness as a function of wavelength, one would see two very similar blackbody curves.

So, there is the electromagnetic spectrum and radiation due to heat (blackbody radiation). But thermal radiation isn't the only way the universe can be observed. How do other kinds of light form?

Photons Light the Way

The part of the universe that is observable is only about 5 percent of the total. This measly fraction includes all of the atoms in the universe. An atom has a nucleus, composed of protons and neutrons, and has a number of electrons equal to the number of protons. If the number of protons and electrons is not the same, then it will either be a positively charged (more protons than electrons) or a negatively charged (more electrons than protons) ion. Most of the light seen in the universe comes from ions.

When an electron is bound to a nucleus, it can be in any of several orbitals, defined by its energy. It's like a satellite orbiting a planet. The closer the satellite is to the planet, the more energy

COSMIC INFLATION EXPLAINED

it would take to move it out of its orbit. Similarly, an electron in a lower orbital requires more energy to be ejected from that state. The lowest energy state is known as the ground state.

Electrons are very picky about where they will and will not go. In order to move from one orbital to another, they must absorb

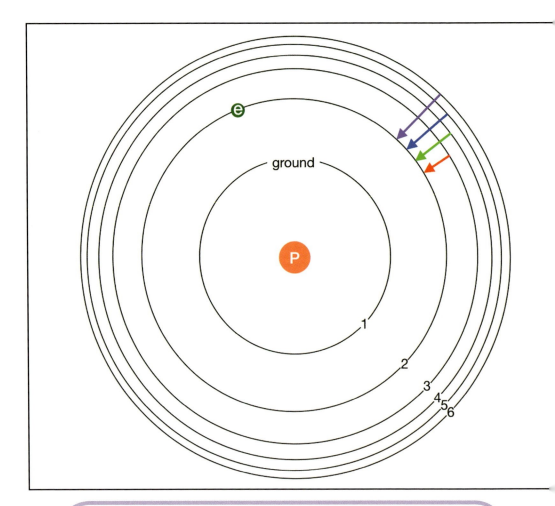

The simplest example of a radiating ion is comprised of a single electron orbiting a single proton. The colored arrows represent the light radiated away when an electron falls down to the second orbital. This is known as the Balmer series.

or emit a specific amount (quantum) of energy in the form of a photon. When an electron absorbs a photon, it goes into a higher energy state. When an electron falls into a lower energy state, it emits a photon. This is the basis for nearly everything observed in the universe.

The image on the left is one of the most common scenarios in the universe: a single electron bound to a single proton. When an electron falls down from a high energy state, for example orbital 6, to a low energy state, orbital 2, it releases a photon with a wavelength in the visible spectrum: purple. Falling from progressively lower energy states (orbitals 5, 4, and 3) to orbital 2 produces progressively lower energy photons, and thus progressively longer wavelengths. This sequence is called the Balmer series. It is commonly used in astronomy to identify and understand things such as star formation and galaxy evolution.

The amount of energy required to move between orbitals is dependent upon how many electrons, protons, and neutrons are in the atom or molecule. Since by definition, this will be different for different compounds, the light radiated from different compounds is unique. This practice is called spectroscopy, and it can help astronomers understand a multitude of astro-physical phenomena.

Breaking Up Light with Spectroscopy

When talking about paints, colors are additive, meaning that if one mixes all of the primary colors of paint together (red, yellow, and blue), one will get a blackish-brownish-greenish color. For light, however, it's the opposite; adding together the primary colors of light (magenta, yellow, and cyan) produces white light.

COSMIC INFLATION EXPLAINED

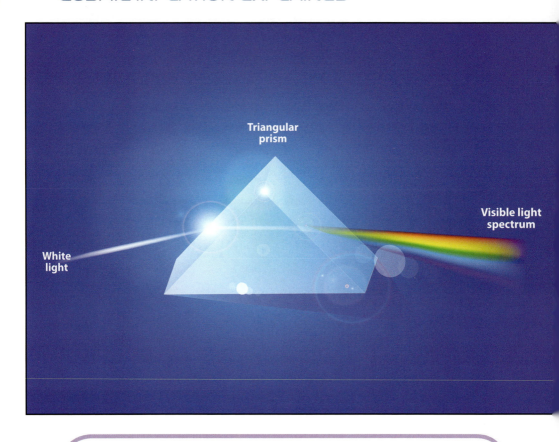

A prism bends incoming white light and produces a rainbow, or spectrum. This is an example of a continuous spectrum.

Spectroscopy breaks up light into its constituent parts, so one can determine the composition of the object.

If you've ever seen a rainbow, you know the basics of spectroscopy. White light comes in and hits either a prism or a diffraction grating. In the case of a rainbow, raindrops in the atmosphere act as a prism, and spread out the white light into the seven colors of the rainbow. The same thing can be done with a diffraction grating, which is a thin piece of plastic that has many

THE 5 PERCENT: HOW DO WE SEE THE UNIVERSE?

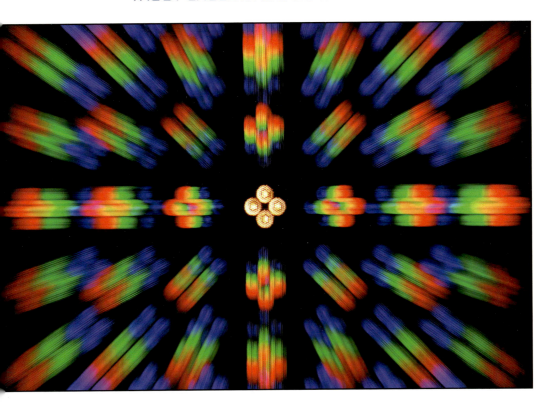

An LED array light goes through a diffraction grating, breaking up white light into its spectrum via a process called diffraction. The white light gets scattered in specific ways, which result in its constituent colors getting spread out. This is an emission spectrum, which tells us what specific elements or molecules are producing the light in the LED.

thousands of scratches in it. The scratches cause the incoming light to bounce in specific ways that enable rainbows, like the one seen in the image above, to form. The back of a CD or DVD is an example of a diffraction grating. If the result of refraction through a prism or diffraction grating is a full rainbow, then this is a continuous spectrum. It is continuous because there are no breaks, or dark lines, in the spectrum.

COSMIC INFLATION EXPLAINED

THE SUN'S SPECTRAL FINGERPRINT

Looking at a spectrum of the sun, one might expect to see a continuous spectrum. The sun emits white light, after all, and is almost entirely a blackbody radiator. However, what a scientist is looking at when she observes the sun with a spectrometer is

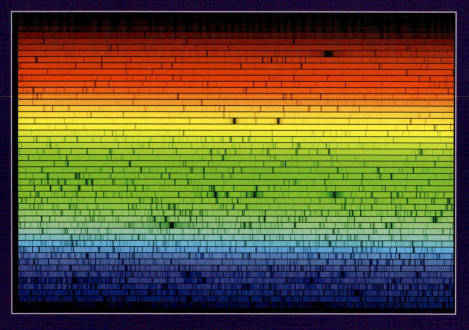

Just like one can determine the composition of light from an LED, one can determine the composition of the sun's photosphere from the set of Fraunhofer lines. These features are a kind of "barcode" that astronomers can use to determine the chemical makeup of the sun's atmosphere. This is an example of an absorption spectrum.

actually the photosphere (the outermost surface of the sun) and its absorption lines superimposed on top. The dark lines in the image correspond to the photosphere's absorption lines and are known as Fraunhofer lines, named after the German astronomer who discovered them, Joseph von Fraunhofer (1787–1826). Absorption lines are essentially the same as emission lines. They correspond to a transition between orbitals, but instead of releasing a photon, these transitions absorb a photon.

Looking at full rainbows isn't the only thing one can do with spectroscopy. Each individual element and molecule has its own "spectral fingerprint." That means that if you look at the light something emits or absorbs with a prism or diffraction grating, you will see a unique pattern of colors (or a unique pattern of dark lines, called absorption lines) for each compound. For example, the image of the LED array light on page 17 shows the chemical composition of the light. This is an example of an emission spectrum. Each of those individual colors can be traced back to a transition from one orbital to another. The colors that are seen provides information about the energy distribution of the orbitals, and thus helps determine the chemical composition of the light. This is fundamentally similar to how astronomers figure out what stars are made of, how they form, how fast they form in galaxies, and even determine the composition of planets outside of our solar system.

Chapter Two

The Other 95 Percent: Dark Matter and Dark Energy

ark matter and dark energy are just that: dark. They can't be directly observed, which means that photons, or light particles, don't interact with dark matter and dark energy. But that doesn't mean they can't be studied; by observing their effects on ordinary matter, scientists can begin to understand what the vast majority of our universe is made of.

The Mystery of Dark Matter

The orbit of any star in a galaxy is very similar to how planets orbit in our solar system. In the solar system, the planets' orbits are nearly circular, with speeds that decrease as one moves further from the central object. If the universe was only comprised of ordinary matter, then one would expect the circular speed of stars in galaxies—including our own—to drop off as one ventures farther and farther from the galaxy's center. In the early seventeenth century, a German scientist and mathematician named Johannes Kepler (1571–1630) devised a set of laws that planets in the solar system seemed to follow. This work was based on very precise observations made by Tycho Brahe (1546–1601). Isaac Newton (1642–1727) improved upon the laws when he formulated the simple description of gravity known today.

Kepler's three laws consider the motions of planets around their host star in ellipses. An ellipse has a long axis, called the major axis, and a short axis, called the minor axis. The semi-major and semi-minor axes are half of these lengths. An ellipse also has two foci, points from which the ellipse can originate. For an orbiting system of bodies, the most massive body (such as the sun) will be at one of the two foci of the ellipse. The closest point in the orbit to the focus is known as the pericenter; the farthest point in the orbit to the focus is known as the apocenter. The period of the orbit is the amount of time it takes to make one complete circuit around. The flatness of the ellipse, or how much the ellipse differs from a circle, is known as the ellipticity. For a circular orbit, the focus is at the center of the orbit; the pericenter, apocenter, semi-major axis, and semi-minor axis are all the same.

COSMIC INFLATION EXPLAINED

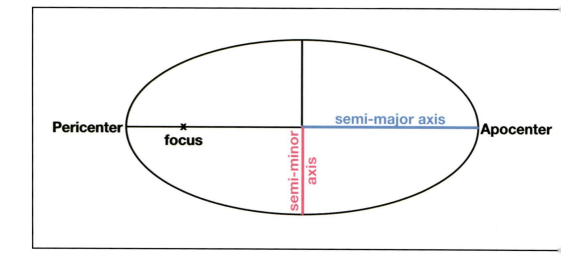

For an elliptical orbit, the massive body will be at one focus. The orbit can then be defined by the peri- and apocenters. The semi-major and semi-minor axes also help to define the ellipse.

Kepler's three laws of planetary motion are as follows:
1. An object orbiting a massive object (such as a planet orbiting a star or a moon orbiting a planet) does so in an ellipse, with the massive object at one focus. The focus is not necessarily the center of the ellipse. If the orbit is perfectly circular (an ellipticity of zero), then the focus is at the circle's center.
2. The area swept out by an orbiting object in a certain amount of time is constant. This means that objects move slower when they're at the far end of their orbit (apocenter) and faster when they're at the closest point in their orbit (pericenter).
3. The square of the period of an orbit is proportional to the cube of its semi-major axis. The constant of proportionality depends on the mass of the two orbiting objects. However, if one measures the time in Earth-years, and the distance in

THE OTHER 95 PERCENT: DARK MATTER AND DARK ENERGY

astronomical units (AU, defined to be the average distance of Earth to the sun), then this constant is exactly one.

Rotation curves of real galaxies show a very different story than the one presented by Kepler. In the region where one would expect the circular speeds to decrease, they appear to stay very nearly constant. This means that there must be some dark material that extends far beyond the visible parts of galaxies, which influences the orbits of stars and removes the observed discrepancy.

VERA RUBIN

One of the main figures in discovering dark matter was Dr. Vera Rubin (1928–2016). Rubin entered the astronomy community at a time when there were very few women in the workforce. She graduated from Vassar College as the only astronomy major in 1948 and then received her master's degree from Cornell University in 1951 and her PhD from Georgetown University in 1954. Rubin taught at Georgetown University until she got a research position at the Carnegie Institute in southern California. There, she worked with W. Kent Ford Jr. (1931–) to observe the spectra of galaxies. She found that in the region of the galaxy where one would expect the circular speeds to decrease, based on Kepler's laws of planetary

(continued on the next page)

COSMIC INFLATION EXPLAINED

(continued from the previous page)

motion, the speeds of stars appeared to stay very nearly constant. Astronomers at the time dubbed this the "galaxy rotation problem," which is solved if one accounts for dark matter. Rubin's discovery completely changed our picture of the universe.[1,2]

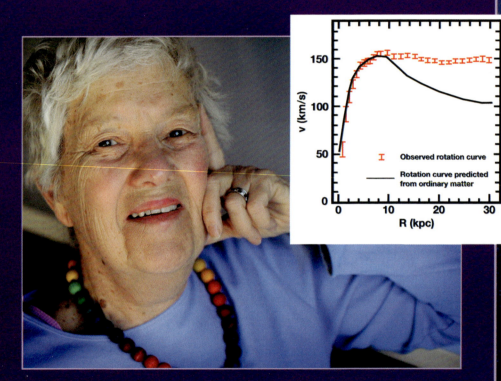

Dr. Vera Rubin was one of the pioneers of modern cosmology. Her major discovery (top right) shows that the observed motions of stars in galaxies do not coincide with their expected speeds. This is direct evidence of dark matter. The horizontal axis is the distance from the center in a distance unit known as kiloparsecs. The vertical axis is the speed of the star in kilometers per second.

THE OTHER 95 PERCENT: DARK MATTER AND DARK ENERGY

One of the most compelling pieces of observational evidence for dark matter is gravitational lensing. Gravity affects everything in the universe, including light—if there's enough mass to bend its path. In that case, the light from a distant object gets bent by a closer object that is nearby or in front of it (typically a cluster of galaxies, or a single massive galaxy), producing a bright distorted image of the background object. In this way, astronomers can see things in the universe that might not have been visible without gravitational lensing. Based on the shape of the images, astronomers can figure out what the distribution of dark matter around the lensing galaxy or galaxy cluster must be.

This is a stunning example of gravitational lensing by the giant cluster of galaxies, Abel 2218. The arcs of light seen throughout the image are actually distant galaxies whose light has been bent by the cluster.

25

This is one of the ways to map out where dark matter is in the universe.[3]

At this point, scientists are convinced that dark matter is a real substance that makes up approximately 27 percent of the universe's mass budget. But what is it exactly? That turns out to be one of the biggest questions in physics right now. Astronomers and physicists are trying to determine what kind of particle (or particles) dark matter is made of at places such as the European Organization for Nuclear Research (CERN) in Switzerland, the High Energy Accelerator Research Organization (KEK) in Japan, and the Sanford Underground Research Facility (SURF) in South Dakota.

Dark Energy Causes Expansion of the Universe

Albert Einstein (1879–1955) showed in 1905 that matter and energy are equivalent, with the famous equation $E = mc^2$, where the constant of proportionality is the speed of light (denoted by c) squared. This implies that mass and energy can be converted into one another.

Dark energy is the energy associated with space itself. It is also known as the vacuum energy, because space is nearly entirely empty. A true vacuum has no material in it (not even air), but space has such a low density of matter that it's essentially a vacuum. Because it exists uniformly everywhere, dark energy is a constant energy field. For that reason, as space expands, the vacuum energy gets stronger, pushing apart everything in the universe. If that sounds confusing, that's because it is. Astronomers and physicists don't fully understand the nature of dark energy. There is a wealth of observational and theoretical evidence in support of dark energy, but it's historically been very difficult to connect the physics of the very small (quantum mechanics, the physics of how atoms form and interact) and the physics of the cosmos (universal expansion and dark energy).[4]

Dark energy causes the universe to expand. If the universe were made up mostly of matter (dark matter and ordinary matter), then one would expect that gravity would eventually win out over the expansion of the universe, thereby slowing the rate at which space expands. However, in 1998, two teams of astronomers (the Supernova Cosmology Project and the High-z Supernova Search Team) independently found the same result: the expansion of the universe is actually accelerating.

The teams measured the accelerated expansion of the universe by looking at Type Ia supernovae, a type of dramatic end to a massive star's life. Type Ia supernovae are formed when a certain kind of star (a white dwarf) explodes to form a neutron star. These explosions release a very specific amount of energy, meaning that all Type Ia supernovae have about the same brightness, called their intrinsic brightness. For this reason, Type Ia supernovae are known in astronomy as "standard candles." Because these objects have the same intrinsic brightness, differences in the *observed* brightness between two Type Ia supernovae are due to differences in their distances. The project that led to the discovery of dark energy was actually very simple; the two teams compared the predicted brightness of many Type Ia supernovae to observations and found that the supernovae were systematically dimmer than predicted—a signature of an accelerating universe, and therefore also of dark energy. Much like the discovery of dark matter, this changed the paradigm for modern cosmology.[5]

COSMIC INFLATION EXPLAINED

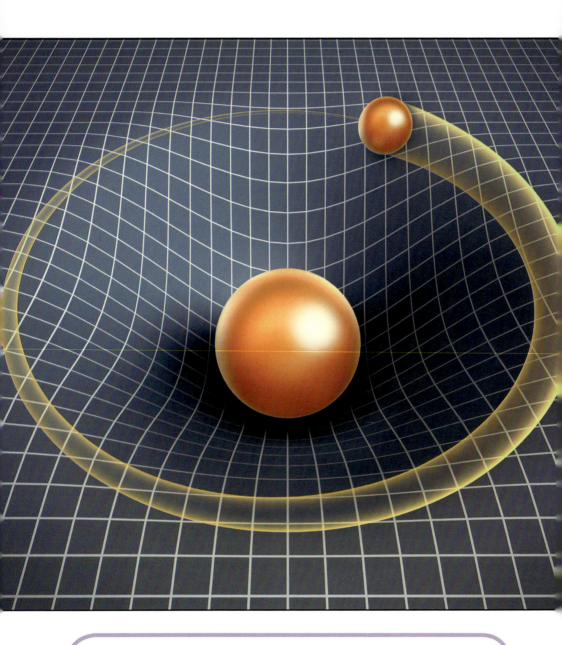

According to general relativity, the fabric of space-time is bent by objects, such as stars and planets. Like a small ball might roll around the dip created by a larger, heavier ball, a planet will orbit its star.

A Universal Puzzle

Newton's formulation of gravity is very simple: objects closer to a central mass are pulled harder toward that mass than something farther away. This isn't the whole picture, however. Einstein's theory of general relativity ties dark matter, ordinary matter, and dark energy together in a fundamental way.

In the simplest terms, Einstein's theory of general relativity states that gravity is actually a geometric effect, kind of like rolling on a hill. Imagine that all of space is like an elastic sheet. Heavier objects (or, more correctly, more massive objects) create larger dips in the sheet. To illustrate the concept, think of a spiral wishing well, or a coin funnel. Coins slowly spiral into the center of the funnel, moving faster as they get closer to the bottom. This is actually a really great analogy to the nature of space under general relativity.

Massive objects create larger dips in the fabric of space, what is often referred to as "the fabric of space-time." This is like the bottom of the funnel. Objects move in orbits around this massive object (or, when more than one massive object is involved, they orbit their common center of mass). The rate at which they orbit is determined by how far away they are from the central object. Smaller objects also create dips in space-time, which can affect the orbits of still smaller things in the system, such as moons. Planets don't spiral into their central star like a coin spirals to the bottom of the funnel because planets don't experience friction as they orbit. Friction causes the coin to lose energy over time, which drives it down toward the bottom of the funnel.

General relativity says that gravity can be described as a geometric effect, as opposed to an actual force. This means

COSMIC INFLATION EXPLAINED

that if scientists can figure out an equation, or set of equations, that define this geometry, they can learn about the nature of space itself. Think of it like making a map. In order to know how to represent a piece of land, one needs to know how tall its mountains are and how deep its oceans go. Mapping out space-time is basically the same thing, but with mathematics.

Einstein figured out the map of space-time in 1915; this is known as the Einstein field equations. Essentially, they say that the geometry—or map—of space-time is dependent upon the amount and distribution of dark energy, dark matter, and ordinary matter. The Einstein field equations also imply that the amount of these three components define the shape of the universe.

Chapter Three

Hubble's Legacy

Before scientists knew about dark matter and dark energy, they were still trying to figure out if the Milky Way was an "island universe," or a galaxy among many. Prior to Edwin Hubble (1889–1953), scientists had observed "fuzzy objects" in the night sky for centuries. Some appeared to be cloud-like objects, and others were spiral shaped. Before Hubble's groundbreaking observations, all of these objects were assumed to be within the Milky Way.

Hubble observed cepheid variable stars in the "spiral nebulae." Cepheid variable stars are stars that have regular cycles of dimming and brightening, the strength of which is related to how bright they can get, or their intrinsic brightness. Because behavior of these stars is so well understood, astronomers are able to measure the distances to these objects directly. In this way, cepheid variable stars are similar to Type Ia supernovae in that they are used as standard candles. From his observations, Hubble was able to figure out the distance to these stars and their host "nebulae." He concluded that the distances were far

Edwin Hubble made the observations that helped the astronomical community realize that the Milky Way galaxy was one among many in our universe.

HUBBLE'S LEGACY

too large to be within the Milky Way, and that the "spiral nebulae" were actually individual galaxies.[1]

Hubble's Law

In addition to telling scientists what the universe is composed of, spectroscopy can also be used to figure out how fast things are moving toward or away from an observer. The most familiar analogy is an ambulance siren. When the ambulance is moving

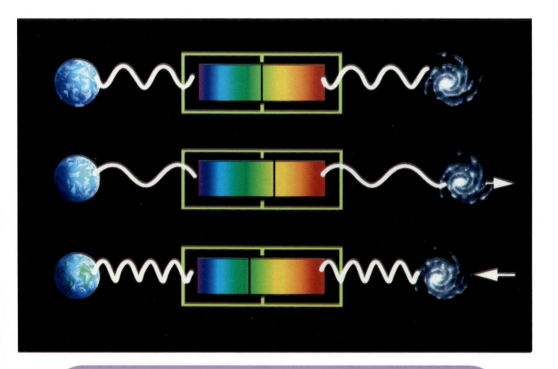

This schematic shows how redshift and blueshift works. The top image shows the observer (Earth) and the object (galaxy) at rest. Light emitted from an object moving away from an observer will appear to have a longer wavelength (or, will be redshifted, middle image). Light emitted from an object moving toward an observer will appear to have a shorter wavelength (or, will be blueshifted, bottom image).

COSMIC INFLATION EXPLAINED

toward you, the pitch of the siren gets higher and higher. As the ambulance moves away from you, the pitch gets progressively lower. This is a phenomenon called the Doppler shift, and it can also be applied to light waves. Since each chemical compound has its own spectral fingerprint, scientists know the emitted wavelengths (or positions of the spectral lines) exactly. Any deviation from those known positions implies movement.

Using these kinds of spectroscopic measurements, Hubble also figured out the velocity of galaxies with respect to our own. He found that there's a nearly linear relationship between recessional velocity (the speed with which something moves away from us, represented by the letter v) and its distance (d) from us. Hubble observed galaxies moving away from our own in every direction he looked on the sky and was the first to find observational evidence for the expansion of the universe. This is known as Hubble's law: $v = H_o d$. The constant H_o is the Hubble constant and gives the rate of expansion. The inverse of the Hubble constant is the Hubble time, which is a pretty good approximation for the age of the universe (roughly 13.7 billion years).

ACTIVITY: WHERE IS THE CENTER OF THE UNIVERSE?

piece of intuition here; it states that there should be no special observers in the universe. If you observe expansion from one point in the universe, then from another point, you should see the same thing. To prove this to yourself, do the following activity:

MATERIALS

- a balloon
- 3 colored markers
- a flexible ruler
- a calculator
- a pencil
- graph paper

DIRECTIONS

1. Pick two points on the balloon to be your "observers." You'll measure all distances from these two points.
2. Draw some "galaxies" on your balloon. Try to distribute them evenly around.
3. On a scratch piece of paper, make a table with two columns: one for each observer.
4. With a partner, blow up the balloon a little bit at a time. Try to blow up the balloon as evenly as possible, as each "blow" corresponds to an expansion interval. Have your partner record the distance from each "observer" to each "galaxy" in the appropriate column.
5. Determine the average distance at each inflation interval by adding up all of the distances and dividing by the total number of distance measurements you made.

(continued on the next page)

COSMIC INFLATION EXPLAINED

(continued from the previous page)

6. On the graph paper (see below), draw an x-axis and label it "Expansion Interval"; this is a time. Draw a y-axis and label it "Average Distance" with the appropriate units that you used in Step 4. You should have two lines: one for each "observer."
7. Plot the averages for each observer. Make sure to keep track of which observer is which by either using a different plotting symbol, or a different color.
8. Make some observations. What do you notice about the two lines? What can you deduce from this activity about the "center" of the universe? See answers on page 72.

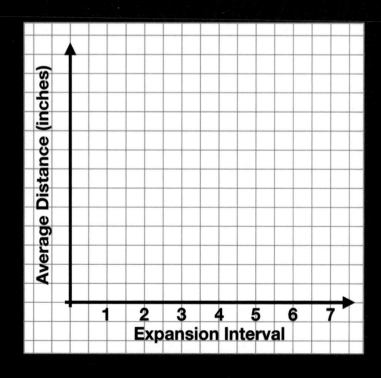

HUBBLE'S LEGACY

The Hubble Space Telescope

Hubble may not have won a Nobel Prize, but he did have one of the most important and influential satellites named after him. The Hubble Space Telescope (HST) has been in orbit around Earth since the early 1990s and is still used by astronomers all over the world.

The original HST had a 2.4-meter (roughly 8-foot) primary mirror, five instruments to look at the universe both spectroscopically and photometrically, and a suite of filters to help astronomers better understand the cosmos. Over the last three decades, the instruments and filter sets have been updated to keep up with new technology. The space shuttle program serviced the Hubble Space Telescope up until 2009, when the program ended.

The first time the Hubble Space Telescope was serviced was in 1993 by astronauts aboard the *Endeavor* space shuttle. Scientists back on Earth discovered that there was something wrong with the Hubble Space Telescope's optics. That is, they noticed the images weren't nearly as sharp as they should be. It turns out there was an issue with the primary mirror on the Hubble Space Telescope: the mirror was ground to the wrong shape. All telescopes have to deal with certain imperfections (called aberrations) in their optics. Some of these aberrations can be alleviated by grinding the mirror to a specific shape. If that shape isn't exactly correct, then the resulting images can be extremely blurry. The Hubble Space Telescope's mirror was off by just over a micrometer. That's smaller than the head of a pin! In order to fix the Hubble Space Telescope, engineers designed something similar to a giant contact lens that fits on top of the primary mirror. Seven astronauts had to receive extensive training

COSMIC INFLATION EXPLAINED

The Hubble Space Telescope orbits Earth approximately fifteen times per day and has been surveying the sky for three decades.

to be able to fix the Hubble Space Telescope's primary mirror, and successfully did so at the tail end of 1993.[2]

Today, the Hubble Space Telescope is still one of the best telescopes available to astronomers around the globe. It has been credited with thousands of discoveries, including the observations that led to the discovery of the rate of expansion of the universe, which won the 2011 Nobel Prize in Physics. The Hubble Space Telescope is far from retirement; it's anticipated that astronomers will still be using the telescope for another twenty years.

Chapter Four

The Far Reaches of the Observable Universe

If the speed of light were infinitely large, then scientists would see all of the stars and galaxies that have ever formed. The night sky would be incredibly bright. This is obviously not the case. The speed of light is a constant (but finite) speed limit in the universe. This implies that looking deeper into the universe is the same as looking back in time. The farthest back that experts are able to observe is known as the cosmic microwave background.

The Cosmic Microwave Background

The cosmic microwave background can be thought of as a baby picture of the universe. Scientists can only see as far back as there is light, and the cosmic microwave background is that edge.

COSMIC INFLATION EXPLAINED

DECADES OF OBSERVING THE COSMIC MICROWAVE BACKGROUND FROM SPACE

Astronomy is a science best performed in space—at least when it comes to observing the universe. That's because Earth's atmosphere blocks out (and traps) a lot of radiation; this is one of the reasons why life is possible on Earth, but it makes observing certain things in the cosmos pretty difficult.

The images on the right show how observations of the cosmic microwave background improved over the last twenty years. In 1989 the first satellite (COBE: COsmic Background Explorer) to measure the cosmic microwave background was launched into space. It measured the temperature of the cosmic microwave background on the whole sky and determined that it was very nearly perfectly isotropic. That means that there is almost no difference in looking at the cosmic microwave background at any point on the sky. Almost. Astronomers did notice that there were small anisotropies. The two lead scientists on COBE, George Smoot (1945–) and John Mather (1946–), won the Nobel Prize in physics in 2006 for their contributions in making cosmology a precision science. Before COBE, astronomers could only theorize about the nature of the universe and make rough estimates based on what could be observed here on Earth. With COBE, so much more was possible.

In 2001, nearly a decade after COBE was decommissioned, the WMAP (Wilkinson Microwave Anisotropy Probe) was launched.

(continued on page 42)

THE FAR REACHES OF THE OBSERVABLE UNIVERSE

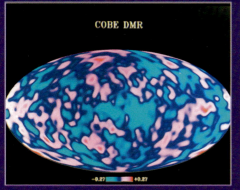
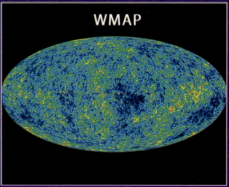
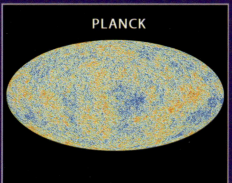

This shows the progression of satellite images of the cosmic microwave background: COBE (*left*), WMAP (*right*), and Planck (*bottom*). The different colors in these images correspond to changes in temperature on the order of 1 part in 100,000.

COSMIC INFLATION EXPLAINED

(continued from page 40)

It had much more sensitive instruments than COBE and was able to determine parameters such as the age of the universe to within one percent!

Astronomers, constantly yearning for better resolution and precision, launched the Planck satellite in 2009. Planck was able to get about three times better resolution than WMAP, and it had at its disposal nine filters in which to observe the cosmic microwave background, as opposed to the five available to WMAP. Planck was also equipped with instruments to measure gravitational lensing of the cosmic microwave background, the Milky Way's dusty material, known as the interstellar medium, and objects within the solar system. The data from Planck has enabled the most precise understanding of the universe and its evolution.

Thanks to the COBE, WMAP, and Planck satellites, physicists know the cosmic microwave background is blackbody radiation from a nearly uniform temperature just under 3 Kelvin (K), but how did it form? What does it say about the formation of the universe?

In the very early universe, protons, electrons, and neutrons were in a hot "soup" known as a plasma. In order for light to be emitted, electrons have to be captured and released from atoms, but if there are no neutral atoms, this process can't happen. At this point, the universe was opaque (we cannot see through it). To understand this better, think of the sun. We can only see its outer atmosphere, the photosphere, not its core. The core is fully ionized, and is thus opaque. The same was true of the universe prior to the formation of the cosmic microwave background. After about three hundred thousand years, the universe was finally cool enough for neutral atoms to form. The first light that can be seen from the universe is the point at which this occurs, often referred to by scientists as the "surface of last scattering," or Recombination. That is the cosmic microwave background radiation.

Ralph Alpher (1921–2007) and Robert Herman (1914–1997) first theorized the cosmic microwave background in 1948, estimating that it would emit blackbody radiation at 5K. The cosmic microwave background fell into astronomical obscurity for nearly two decades until the study of cosmology became more popular. In 1964 two astronomers, Arno Penzias (1933–) and Robert Woodrow Wilson (1936–), at Bell Telephone

In the early 1960s, Robert Woodrow Wilson (*left*) and Arno Penzias (*right*) accidentally discovered the cosmic microwave background at Bell Telephone Laboratories.

COSMIC INFLATION EXPLAINED

Laboratories accidentally discovered the cosmic microwave background. They were hoping to measure the radio emission from the Milky Way. In every direction they pointed their antennae, they measured blackbody radiation with a temperature of about 4K, which they couldn't explain with background radiation from Earth. They concluded that the noise in their data had to be of extragalactic origin, and was likely the cosmic microwave background. Their discovery won them the 1978 Nobel Prize in physics.[1]

How Did the Universe Get Here?

Once the cosmic microwave background was really taken seriously in the scientific community, there were two main theories for how the universe began. One theory was that the universe was always here, and it had been evolving the same way for all of time. Though it seems appealing from a philosophical point of view, this theory couldn't explain the observations seen in the universe today and in the recent past. The other idea is known as the big bang theory. This states that the universe started out as a singularity, an infinitely small point that was infinitely dense and infinitely hot. This theory had several advantages; it could explain Hubble's law, large-scale structure (such as the formation of galaxy groups and clusters), and the relative amounts of light elements, such as hydrogen and helium.

The cosmic microwave background is direct evidence for the big bang theory. The cosmic microwave background has very nearly the same temperature everywhere on the sky. In order for that to happen, all points on the sky must have at some time

44

THE FAR REACHES OF THE OBSERVABLE UNIVERSE

Expanding Universe

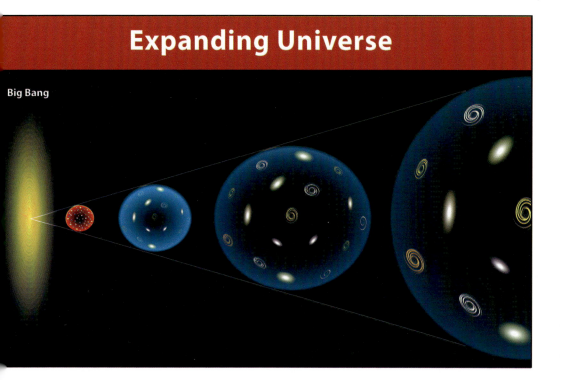

The big bang theory postulates that the universe began as an infinitesimally small point and rapidly grew to its present size.

in the past been "causally connected." That means that two points on opposite parts of the sky had to be close enough to affect one another. The only way for this to have occurred is if the universe started off extremely small and grew to the size it is today. It may seem a little far-fetched, but so far this is the best theory for the universe's explosive beginnings.

Chapter Five

Cosmic Inflation: Something from Nothing

If we accept that the universe started as an explosion from an infinitely dense, infinitely hot point (that is, the big bang), then we need to understand how the cosmos got to be the size it is today. Much of this process is due to cosmic inflation. First described by MIT physicist Alan Guth in the 1970s, it is widely accepted as the correct counterpart to the big bang theory by cosmologists because it solves three of its biggest problems: the horizon problem, the flatness problem, and the monopole problem.

The Horizon Problem

As previously discussed, the cosmic microwave background is almost entirely isotropic. Since information (such as temperature) can't travel faster than the speed of light, one wouldn't necessarily expect parts of the sky that are light-years apart to have the same temperature. This means that the universe must have started off much smaller and undergone a period of rapid expansion. Another piece to the horizon problem is that Earth does not exist at some special place in the universe. If one were to travel to a part of the universe thirteen billion light years away, the cosmic microwave background should look the same as it does here. This is only possible if cosmic inflation produced an incredibly large universe, much larger than the observable horizon.

The Flatness Problem

The amount of dark energy, dark matter, and ordinary matter affect the geometry of the universe. The density of some object is its mass divided by the volume it takes up. The same thing can be done for the density of dark energy, dark matter, and ordinary matter in the universe. By comparing the sum of these three densities (that is, adding together the densities of dark energy, dark matter, and ordinary matter) to a critical density, one can figure out the shape, or "curvature," of the universe.

Astronomers have determined that the universe is flat by doing just that. They can figure out the *current* density of dark matter, dark energy, and ordinary matter from the cosmic microwave background. The relative amount of dark matter, dark energy, and ordinary matter has changed over the lifetime of the universe. The fact that the universe is flat today means that it must have always been flat. This is the heart of the flatness problem. Any tiny fluctuation in the density of the universe would have been hugely amplified over the history of the universe (that's what is seen with the cosmic microwave background and the formation

COSMIC INFLATION EXPLAINED

These are the possible shapes of the universe: flat (*left*), closed (*middle*), or open (*right*).

of large structures of galaxies). Thus, it seems almost too good to be true that the universe began with *just the right* density such that it is observed to be flat, even today.

Cosmic inflation removes this "fine tuning" problem. With a period of rapid expansion just after the big bang, any value of the density of the universe would have been driven toward the critical density. Consider living on the surface of a balloon (like your balloon "universe" in the activity from Chapter 2). If you're fairly big with respect to the size of the balloon, then you'd realize that the balloon was round. But if the balloon were inflated to the size of Earth, or even larger astronomical scales, then your horizon would appear flat, no matter where you looked. This is essentially what happened during the period of cosmic inflation.

COSMIC INFLATION: SOMETHING FROM NOTHING

The Magnetic Monopole Problem

Positive and negative charges are independent; it's easy to find a positive charge without a negative charge (such as a proton), just as it's easy to find a negative charge without a positive charge (such as an electron). These are called electric monopoles, because there's only one sign associated with each particle. In contrast, a magnet has two poles: a north and south pole.

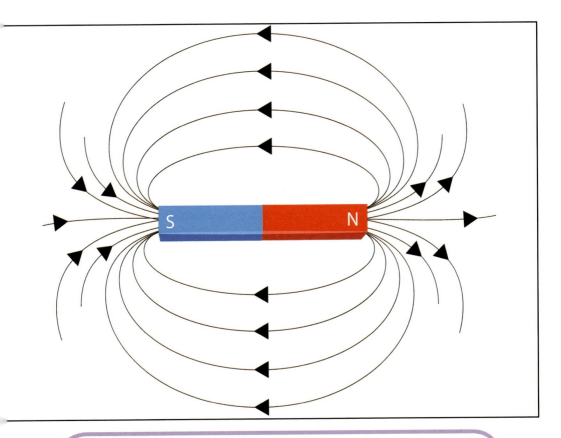

Magnetic field lines exit magnets at the north pole, and enter at the south pole, as shown by the arrows in this image. If one were to cut this magnet in half, one would have two nearly identical magnets. All magnets known on Earth have two poles.

COSMIC INFLATION EXPLAINED

If you cut a bar magnet in half, you get two nearly identical bar magnets, each with its own north and south pole. If electricity and magnetism are so related, why should it be that we don't see any magnetic monopoles in the universe?

It turns out that magnetic monopoles are incredibly difficult to create: you need extremely high temperatures and pressures to form them. The only time in the history of the universe when these criteria were met was just after the big bang. The magnetic monopole problem is this: if magnetic monopoles could have been formed in the very early universe, why haven't any been observed today? Cosmic inflation again solves this problem. Even if a few magnetic monopoles managed to form just after the big bang, cosmic inflation would have hugely expanded the space in which they exist, making the density of magnetic monopoles extremely low. The probability of observing a magnetic mono-pole is then very small, consistent with what is observed today.[1]

What Caused Cosmic Inflation?

What exactly caused the universe to rapidly expand so soon after the big bang? This is actually one of the biggest open questions in astronomy. The prevailing theory has to do with fields. To understand what a field is, imagine a charged particle. The electric field around a positive charge looks something like in the image on the right page. The arrows are called field lines, and they trace out the electric field. For a positive charge (top panel), these field lines always point away from the origin. If instead there is a negative charge (as in the bottom panel), the field lines point toward the origin. Thus, the field lines all have a direction (toward or away from the origin) and a magnitude (often depicted as the length of the arrows) that corresponds to how

50

COSMIC INFLATION: SOMETHING FROM NOTHING

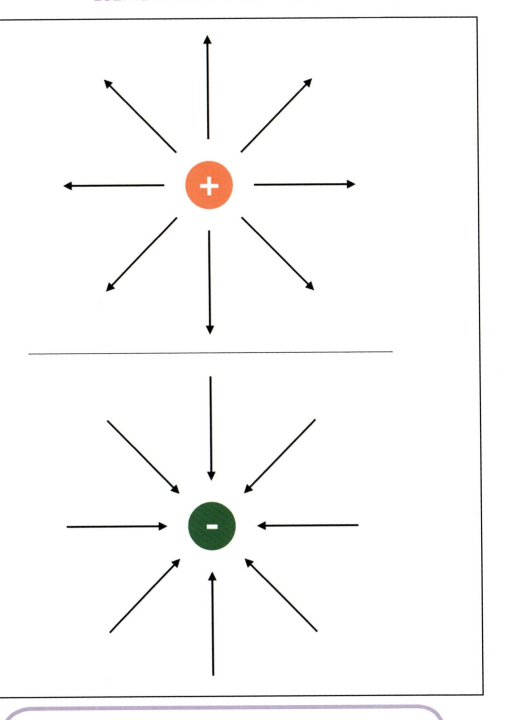

This shows the electric field from an isolated positive charge (*top*) and an isolated negative charge (*bottom*). These are an example of a vector field.

COSMIC INFLATION EXPLAINED

negative or positive the charge is. Anything in physics that has both a direction and a magnitude is known as a vector. Another vector is velocity, where the magnitude (or the velocity's scalar component) is the speed. In this way, we can call the electric field a vector field. If the field only has a magnitude, then we call it a scalar field. One scalar field is temperature. Everything in the universe has a temperature (even if it's really cold!), but temperature doesn't have any directionality.

Physicists think that there was a scalar field, called the inflaton field, that drove the rapid expansion of the universe during cosmic inflation. The theory goes that the inflaton field

SCIENTIFIC NOTATION

Scientists typically run into numbers that are either too big or too small to write out all of the zeros before or after the decimal point (called decimal notation). To avoid confusion, numbers are written in terms of how many factors of ten go into them. This is explained visually in the examples on the right: move the decimal point over to the right when the number is less than one, or over to the left when the number is greater than one, to find the base number. The number of times you've moved the decimal point over will be the number in the exponent, with a sign that corresponds to whether you moved the decimal point to the right (negative) or to the left (positive).

COSMIC INFLATION: SOMETHING FROM NOTHING

$$0.00004$$

$$4 \times 10^{-5}$$

$$380000.0$$

$$3.8 \times 10^{5}$$

The table below gives several examples of a decimal number with its corresponding scientific notation. In physics and astronomy, scientists make measurements in various different units, such as meters and seconds. They often want to describe these with words, and to do so, they can attach a prefix to the unit of measure. If, for example, one measures an object to be 0.305 meters long, one could write that it is 3.05 decimeters, 30.5 centimeters, or 305 millimeters in length. Using these different prefixes makes it easier to compare values for individual observations.

Prefix	Decimal Notation	Scientific Notation
nano	0.000000001	10^{-9}
micro	0.000001	10^{-6}
milli	0.001	10^{-3}
centi	0.01	10^{-2}
deci	0.1	10^{-1}
kilo	1,000	10^{3}
mega	1,000,000	10^{6}
giga	1,000,000,000	10^{9}

COSMIC INFLATION EXPLAINED

was formed during the big bang and was *just barely* stable—a phenomenon physicists call a metastable state. To understand this, consider taking a bottle of distilled water and placing it in a freezer. Normally, one would expect the bottle of water to just turn to ice. However, if the distilled water is left undisturbed, then it can remain a liquid even below its freezing point of 32°F (0°C). This is known as supercooled water. If suddenly you tap the bottle of supercooled water, then you can watch ice crystals form in a matter of seconds.[2] Something similar happened to the inflaton field: when the strong nuclear force decoupled from the other fundamental forces, there was a huge release of energy which may have disrupted the metastable inflaton field enough to trigger inflation. The transition of the inflaton field from the metastable state, which started about 10^{-36} seconds after the big bang, drove cosmic inflation, and lasted until about 10^{-12} seconds after the big bang. Once this happened, the particles associated with the inflaton field decayed rapidly, producing the particles observed today.[3]

Chapter Six

The Past, Present, and Future of Our Universe

Immediately after the big bang, the four fundamental forces (gravity, the electromagnetic force, and the strong and weak nuclear forces) were unified together in one. Gravity is the most familiar of the fundamental forces, as it is the force that holds us to the ground and causes planets to orbit stars. Everything from light to electricity is mediated by the electromagnetic force. The strong nuclear force is responsible for holding atoms together, while the weak nuclear force governs interactions between atoms and molecules. Scientists think gravity was the first to "freeze out," or become distinguishable from the other forces, at 10^{-43} seconds after the big bang, followed by the strong nuclear force, which may have triggered cosmic inflation. This is as close to the beginning of the universe as astronomers and physicists can theorize.

One Force Becomes Four

Until about 10^{-36} seconds after the big bang, massive particles are continuously created and destroyed (or annihilated) by their antiparticle pair. Antiparticles are identical to their particle counterparts, but have an opposite charge. When a particle and antiparticle pair interact, they annihilate one another and generate an amount of energy equivalent to their combined mass. This is possible because mass and energy are equivalent. Cosmic inflation occurs at 10^{-36} seconds after the big bang and lasts until about 10^{-12} seconds. During this time, the universe becomes flat and astronomically large. The strong nuclear force decouples from the weak nuclear and electromagnetic forces, and joins gravity as a separate force. It isn't until 10^{-12} seconds after the big bang that there are four distinguishable forces.

Nuclear Fusion and Recombination

Ten seconds after the big bang, all of the particles and antiparticles that the universe will ever have are created. For about three minutes, nuclear fusion, the process that powers the cores of stars, occurs to form elements other than hydrogen. By four minutes after the big bang, the universe is too cool to run fusion, and what is left is about 75 percent hydrogen, 25 percent helium, and very small amounts of heavier elements and isotopes such as deuterium, lithium, and beryllium.

The universe at this point in time is a plasma of atomic nuclei, electrons, and photons. Photons can barely travel anywhere before being absorbed and reemitted by nearby ions. Once the universe becomes cool enough, free electrons combine with ionized nuclei to form neutral atoms, and the universe becomes transparent. The moment at which this occurs is called recombination, and the surface seen as a result of this is the cosmic microwave background.

The Dark Ages

There is a period of about twenty-five thousand years between recombination and the formation of the first stars and galaxies, known as the Dark Ages, for which there is very little information about the state of the universe. Since there were no (or very few) stars, there was no light to provide information about the local conditions. The farthest scientists have been able to probe is a galaxy at about four hundred million years after the big bang. This galaxy formed just after the end of the Dark Ages; it is about a quarter the size and one one-hundredth the mass of the Milky Way, but it is forming stars twenty times as fast as our galaxy is.[1] Typically, astronomers use objects known as quasars to observe the very early universe. Quasars are the cores of incredibly massive galaxies. They are the brightest objects in the universe, which is why they're the perfect tools for understanding early times after the big bang.

The Fate of the Universe

For most of the lifetime of the universe, space-time has been expanding at a relatively constant rate. The relative amounts of dark energy, dark matter, and ordinary matter are not constant. About 8.5 billion years after the big bang, the universe became dominated by dark energy and began a period of accelerated expansion that is still underway.

So, what's in store for our universe? The answer to this question depends on the geometry of space-time. In a closed

Now
13,700,000,000 YEARS
AFTER BIG BANG

DARK ENERGY?

FORMATION OF
THE SOLAR SYSTEM
8,700,000,000 YEARS
AFTER BIG BANG

GALAXY EVOLUTION
CONTINUES...

FIRST GALAXIES
1000,000,000 YEARS
AFTER BIG BANG

FIRST STARS
400,000,000 YEARS
AFTER BIG BANG

THE DARK AGES

COSMIC MICROWAVE
BACKGROUND
400,000 YEARS AFTER
BIG BANG

INFLATION

THE
BIG
BANG

Just after the formation of the cosmic microwave background, there were no stars to illuminate space. Thus, the span of time between the formation of the cosmic microwave background and the formation of the first stars is known as the Dark Ages.

THE PAST, PRESENT, AND FUTURE OF OUR UNIVERSE

universe, eventually the universe would become so massive that gravity would win out over expansion, causing what's called a "big crunch." Eventually, temperatures, pressures, and densities would reach values similar to the big bang, perhaps "restarting" the universe. In an open universe, it may be possible for the amount of dark energy to greatly increase with time. If this were to happen, expansion due to dark energy would rip apart structures such as galaxies and even solar systems: this is known as the "big rip."

HOW DO STARS FORM AND EVOLVE?

Stars form out of clouds of gas and dust, known as giant molecular clouds. These clouds must be relatively cool in order for molecular hydrogen (H_2) to form. Once there's enough material, the cloud will begin to break into smaller pieces, or fragment. The pieces will slowly collapse on themselves, due to their own gravity, and gradually get hotter. Eventually, at the very center of this clump of material, the temperature and pressure gets high enough for nuclear fusion to begin, and a star is officially formed. Nuclear fusion is the process by which any element other than hydrogen is formed.

In the most massive stars, nuclear fusion occurs very early on in their lifetimes, and ends relatively quickly. These stars (known as O and A supergiants) live fast and die young, producing some of the

(continued on the next page)

COSMIC INFLATION EXPLAINED

(continued from the previous page)

Molecular clouds are clouds of dust and gas. Sometimes called "stellar nurseries," molecular clouds are where stars are born. This particular cloud can be found in the constellation Orion, and is actually visible under dark sky conditions with a small telescope or binoculars.

brightest events in the observable universe: supernovae. The least massive stars (K, M, L, T, and Y dwarfs) fuse as much material in their cores as they can before they become too cool for fusion to continue. These dwarfs don't die in a spectacular way; they cool on time periods often much longer than the age of the universe. Our star, the sun, is a pretty average star. It formed about 4.6 billion years ago, and in another 4.6 billion years, it will eventually blow off its outer layers, forming a planetary nebula. The remnants of evolved stars return gas and dust back into the universe, providing the material for more stars to form.

THE PAST, PRESENT, AND FUTURE OF OUR UNIVERSE

It seems far more likely, however, that the amount of dark energy will stay constant with time. In that event, and given the fact that information from the cosmic microwave background indicates that our universe is flat, we will likely experience what is called the "big freeze." In this scenario, the universe expands at an increasing rate for the rest of time. Eventually, the space between galaxies will become immeasurably large, stars will run out of the fuel necessary to form, and the universe will cool and grow darker with time, until its inevitable heat death.[2]

Unanswered Questions in Cosmology

From the preceding chapters, it may seem like scientists have a complete understanding of cosmology and our universe. That is far from true. There are still many questions left unanswered, the answers to which will only become apparent with creative and inquisitive minds working on their solutions. The following are just a few examples of what remains to be known about our universe.

Dark Matter Particle

When astronomers first started really trying to understand the nature of dark matter, they first tried to explain the "missing mass," with different kinds of ordinary matter. Among these candidates were brown dwarfs (failed stars due to their low masses), dead stars, black holes, and neutrinos. Eventually it became apparent that dark matter had to be a new kind of material that astronomers and physicists alike had never seen before. The prevailing theory is that dark matter is a fundamental particle, like a proton or electron, but one that only interacts with the rest of the universe via gravity.[1] That means it doesn't emit or absorb any light. Because it does not experience any interactions with the electromagnetic spectrum, it appears completely dark.

The standard model of particle physics attempts to describe how the universe is structured on the very smallest scales. This model fully describes how three of the four fundamental forces (the strong and weak nuclear forces, and electromagnetism) work. Unfortunately, its description of gravity is still incomplete. Some of its biggest failings are that it does not include a dark matter particle, is incompatible with our understanding of gravity under general relativity, and does not account for dark energy. Particle physicists have come up with a slight modification to the standard model, called supersymmetry, which might bridge the gap between our current understanding of the universe and a more complete model of gravity. Each particle in the standard model would have a much more massive supersymmetric counterpart (so-called "sparticles"). Physicists are attempting to create these sparticles in extremely high-energy particle collisions at CERN, but have yet to find any supersymmetric candidates.

Another potential candidate for the dark matter particle is known as a weakly interacting massive particle, or WIMP.

COSMIC INFLATION EXPLAINED

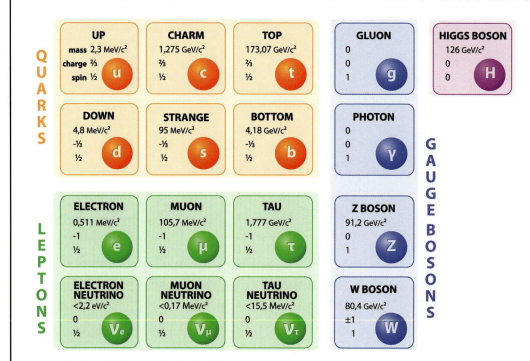

These are all the particles included in the standard model of particle physics. Quarks make up subatomic particles like protons and neutrons. Leptons are formed in very energetic events in the universe and are commonly referred to as "cosmic rays." Gauge bosons mediate the fundamental forces. Finally, the Higgs boson is what physicists believe gives objects in the universe mass.

One of the ways physicists have been searching for WIMPs is by scanning the night sky for intense bursts of gamma ray radiation, which might be a sign of dark matter self-annihilation. That means that whatever dark matter particle there might be would need to have a nearby corresponding antiparticle. The interaction between these two would destroy both particles,

UNANSWERED QUESTIONS IN COSMOLOGY

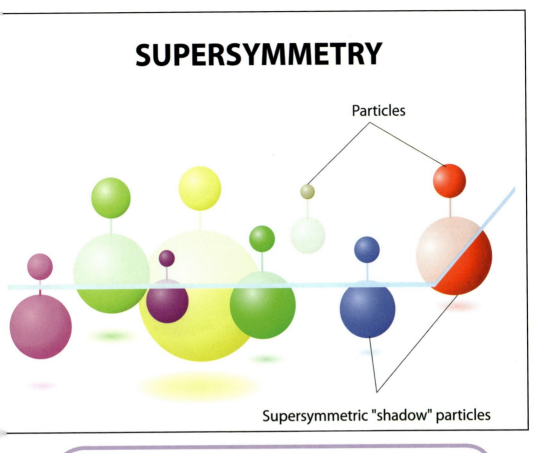

The theory of supersymmetry predicts that for every particle there is a more massive supersymmetric particle. This theory also predicts a supersymmetric dark matter particle which would account for the "missing mass" seen in astronomical observations.

producing a large burst of light. Other scientists have attempted to observe WIMPs directly, using large detectors. The thought is that even though these particles should pass directly through Earth without interacting with anything, there may be a slight build up of less energetic WIMPs in a large enough detector over a long enough period of time. So far, both direct and indirect detection for WIMPs has been unsuccessful.

The Nature of Dark Energy

As previously discussed, dark energy is an unknown type of energy associated with space itself. It is thought to be uniformly distributed throughout all space and responsible for the accelerated expansion of the universe that began roughly five billion years ago. Though astronomers have clear evidence for its effects, they have yet to really understand the source and nature of dark energy.

Quantum Gravity

A theory of quantum gravity is necessary in order to reconcile the very large scale (gravity and general relativity) with the very small scale (quantum mechanics). An atomic nucleus is dominated by the strong nuclear force, so much so that effects due to gravity don't matter at all. But gravity is the force that holds the universe together—is this at odds with what we experience every day? It turns out, it's not. On the scales of atomic nuclei, the strong nuclear force is one hundred thousand trillion trillion trillion times stronger than gravity.[2] That's one followed by forty-one zeros. Another mystery in modern physics is why gravity is so much weaker than all of the other fundamental forces.

The theory of cosmic inflation actually requires that quantum gravity exist. Though the cosmic microwave background is nearly completely isotropic, there are tiny discrepancies that are thought to originate from quantum fluctuations in the very early universe. These tiny fluctuations have been amplified over time, producing the groups and clusters of galaxies observed today. Theories of quantum gravity are needed to explain how the universe behaved when it was only 10^{-36} seconds old.

Galaxy clusters are the most massive structures in the universe. Nearly every point (or blob) seen in this image is a galaxy that belongs to a single cluster: Abell 1689. Galaxy clusters can contain several to hundreds of thousands of galaxies. Our Milky Way belongs to a much smaller cluster than the one shown here, made up of several hundred galaxies.

COSMIC INFLATION EXPLAINED

Beyond the Observable

During the period of cosmic inflation, space itself expanded at a rate faster than the speed of light. As discussed in Chapter 4, part of the solution to the horizon problem is that the universe expanded to such a large volume during cosmic inflation that even if you travel to the farthest reaches of our observable universe, you would still see essentially the same cosmic microwave background radiation. But the cosmic microwave background is not completely homogeneous and isotropic. This could mean that there are some regions of space that have an over density of matter — and these regions might not be within our visible horizon. Astronomers have observed a slight preference in speed and direction of the motion of massive clusters. They theorize that this could be due to the gravitational influence of material no longer within our visible universe.

CHAPTER NOTES

Chapter One

The 5 Percent: How Do We See the Universe?

1. "Planck's New Cosmic Recipe," *European Space Agency*, updated May 11, 2015, sci.esa.int/planck/51557-planck-new-cosmic-recipe.

Chapter Two

The Other 95 Percent: Dark Matter and Dark Energy

1. Steven Soter and Neil deGrasse Tyson, eds., *Cosmic Horizons: Astronomy at the Cutting Edge*, New York, NY: New Press, 2000, http://www.amnh.org/explore/resource-collections/cosmic-horizons/profile-vera-rubin-and-dark-matter.
2. "Women in Aviation and Space History: Vera Cooper Rubin," Smithsonian National Air and Space Museum, accessed November 30, 2017, https://airandspace.si.edu/explore-and-learn/topics/women-in-aviation/rubin.cfm.
3. "Detailed Dark Matter Map Yields Clues to Galaxy Cluster Growth," NASA, November 12, 2010, https://www.nasa.gov/mission_pages/hubble/science/dark-matter-map.html.
4. Ethan Siegel, "No, Dark Energy Isn't an Illusion," *Forbes*, April 11, 2017, https://www.forbes.com/sites/startswithabang/2017/04/11/no-dark-energy-isnt-an-illusion.

COSMIC INFLATION EXPLAINED

5. Rebecca Boyle, "Dark Energy Wins Nobel Price in Physics," *Popular Science,* October 4, 2011, https://www.popsci.com/science/article/2011-10/dark-energy-discovery-wins-physics-nobel.

Chapter Three
Hubble's Legacy

1. "Edwin P. Hubble," NASA, accessed November 30, 2017, https:// asd.gsfc.nasa.gov/archive/hubble/overview/hubble_bio.html.

2. "History: The Spherical Aberration Problem," Hubble Space Telescope, accessed November 30, 2017, http://www.spacetelescope.org/about/history/aberration_problem/.

Chapter Four
The Far Reaches of the Observable Universe

1. "This Month in Physics History - June 1963: Discovery of Cosmic Microwave Background," *American Physical Society News* 11, no. 7 (July 2002), accessed November 30, 2017, http://www.aps.org/publications/apsnews/200207/history.cfm.

Chapter Five
Cosmic Inflation: Something from Nothing

1. T'mir Danger Julius, "The Mysterious Missing Magnetic Monopole," Phys Org, August 9, 2016, https://phys.org/news/2016-08-mysterious-magnetic-monopole.html.

70

2. Veritasium, "Supercooled Water - Explained!" YouTube, March 22, 2011, http://www.youtube.com/watch?v=ph8xusY3GTM.

3. Gary Scott Watson, "Inflation and Scalar Fields," An Exposition on Inflationary Cosmology, NASA/IPAC Extragalactic Database (NED), accessed November 30, 2017, http://ned.ipac.caltech.edu/level5/Watson/Watson5_3.html.

Chapter Six
The Past, Present, and Future of Our Universe

1. Ashley Morrow, "Hubble Team Breaks Cosmic Distance Record," NASA, March 3 2016, www.nasa.gov/feature/goddard/2016/hubble-team-breaks-cosmic-distance-record.

2. Clara Moskowitz, "Endless Void or Big Crunch: How Will the Universe End?" Space.com, October 26, 2011, http://www.space.com/13393-universe-endless-void-big-crunch.html.

Chapter Seven
Unanswered Questions in Cosmology

1. Gianfranco Bertone, "How Dark Matter Became a Particle," *CERN Courier,* April 13, 2017, http://cerncourier.com/cws/article/cern/68432.

2. Fermilab, "Quantum Gravity," YouTube, February 2, 2016, http://www.youtube.com/watch?v=CbPWYjnQIO8.

COSMIC INFLATION EXPLAINED

Answer to activity on page 34

If you have evenly spaced your "expansion intervals," then the two lines should be both linear and parallel. This means that no matter where you sit on the balloon, you'll see objects moving away from you at the same rate. From this, we can conclude that there is no "center" to the universe.

GLOSSARY

absolute zero The concept of "absolute zero" is when there is no energy for motion, even at the atomic scale. This is the basis for the unit of temperature Kelvin (K).

antiparticle A subatomic particle that is identical to its regular particle counterpart, but with an opposite charge. For example, a positron is the antiparticle to the electron and has a positive charge.

big bang theory The theory for how the universe began, which states that all of the material in the universe that can (and cannot) be seen originated from an infinitely hot, infinitely dense, and infinitely small point.

Cepheid variable star A star that has a pulsating brightness that varies in a well-understood way.

diffraction grating A thin piece of plastic with tiny scratches on it, which can break up white light into its constituent parts.

electron A subatomic particle with a negative charge. The electron is about two thousand times less massive than a proton.

Fraunhofer lines The absorption lines observed in the sun's atmosphere.

ground state The lowest, most stable energy state in an atom or molecule.

homogeneous Having the same composition throughout.

ion An atom or molecule with an unequal amount of protons and electrons.

isotope An atom or molecule with more neutrons than is typically found in nature. These are more massive than their natural counterparts, and for that reason are typically called "heavy."

COSMIC INFLATION EXPLAINED

isotropic Appearing the same in every direction.

linear Describes the very simple relationship between the x and y variables that when plotted, looks like a straight line.

monopole A point from which field lines either all point toward or away.

neutron A subatomic particle with electric charge. The neutron is about as massive as the proton.

observable horizon The limit to how far back in the universe's life scientists can observe.

orbital The energy states of an electron around an atom or molecule.

parallel Two lines are said to be parallel if they have the same slope, but not necessarily the same y-intercept.

photometry The practice of collecting photons.

photon A light particle.

photosphere The outermost layer of the sun's atmosphere.

prism A piece of glass that breaks white light into its constituent parts.

proton A subatomic particle with a positive charge. The number of protons defines an element.

quantum A specific amount.

quantum mechanics A field of physics that attempts to understand how objects behave at the subatomic level.

quasar The incredibly bright nucleus of a distant galaxy.

recombination The period of time roughly four hundred thousand years after the big bang, when electrons combined with protons and neutrons to create neutral atoms.

scalar Describes a measurement that has only magnitude.

singularity An infinitely small point.

GLOSSARY

slope The rate of change of a straight line, often written as the letter "b."

vacuum A region of space that has no (or very few) atoms and/or molecules in it.

vector A measurement that has both a magnitude (scalar component) and direction.

y-intercept The location at which any function (whether it be linear, quadratic, parabolic, or something else) crosses the y-axis.

FURTHER READING

Books

Ansdell, Megan. *The Big Bang Explained.* New York, NY: Enslow Publishing, 2019.

Cham, Jorge, and Daniel Whiteson. *We Have No Idea: A Guide to the Unknown Universe*. New York, NY: Riverhead Publishing, 2017.

DK. *Space!* New York, NY: DK Publishing, 2015.

Levin, Janna. *Black Hole Blues and Other Songs From Outer Space*. New York, NY: Anchor Publishing, 2017.

May, Brian. *STEM Guide to the Universe: Exploring the Mysteries of the Universe*. New York, NY: Rosen Publishing, 2016.

Pamplona, Alberto Hernandez. *Visual Exploration of Science: A Visual Guide to the Universe*. New York, NY: Rosen Publishing, 2017.

Tyson, Neil deGrasse. *Death by Black Hole and Other Cosmic Quandaries*. New York, NY: W. W. Norton & Company, Inc. Publishing, 2014.

FURTHER READING

Websites

Amazing Space

amazingspace.org

Hosted by the Hubble Space Telescope, this website will be your guide to the past, current, and future space telescope missions.

Khan Academy

www.khanacademy.org/science/cosmology-and-astronomy

These video tutorials guide you through the basics and give you the tools necessary to understand more complex topics in cosmology and astronomy.

Space Scoop

www.spacescoop.org/en/

Stay current in astronomy news!

INDEX

A

antiparticles, 56, 64
astronomers, 6–8, 18–19, 21–27, 31–34, 37–38, 39–44, 68

B

balloons, 8, 35–36, 48, 72
big bang theory, 8, 9, 44–45, 46, 50, 54, 55–59
blackbody radiation, 10–13, 42–44

C

cepheid variable stars, 31
cosmic inflation, 8, 26–27, 34, 46–54, 56, 59, 66–68
cosmic microwave background, 39–45, 46–48, 57–58, 61, 66–68

D

Dark Ages, 57
dark energy, 20, 26–27, 29–30, 47, 57–59, 66
dark matter, 20–30, 47, 57, 62–65
decimal notation, 52–53

E

diffraction grating, 16–17, 19
Doppler shift, 34

Egypt, ancient, 6–7
Einstein, Albert, 26, 29–30
electromagnetic spectrum, 10–11, 63
electrons, 13–15, 42, 56, 63
expansion, cosmic, 8, 26–27, 34, 46–54, 56, 59, 66–68
Expansion Interval activity, 34–36, 72

F

flatness problem, 46–48
Fraunhofer lines, 18–19

G

galaxies
  clusters of, 25–26, 66–68
  quasars in, 57
  recessional velocity of, 34
galaxy rotation problem, 24
general relativity, 28–30, 63, 66
gravitational lensing, 25
gravity, 21, 25, 29, 55, 59, 63, 66
ground state, 14
Guth, Alan, 8, 46

INDEX

H

heat, 10–13
horizon problem, 46–47, 68
Hubble, Edwin, 31–34, 37–38, 44
Hubble's Law, 33–34, 44
Hubble Space Telescope, 37–38

I

inflation, cosmic, 8, 26–27, 34, 46–54, 56, 59, 66–68
inflaton field, 52–54
ions, 13–14, 56

K

Kepler, Johannes, 21–23

L

light, 10–19, 25, 33–34, 42–43, 63

M

magnetic monopoles, 49–50
matter, dark, 20–30, 47, 57, 62–65
microwave background, cosmic, 39–45, 46–48, 57–58, 61, 66–68
microwaves, 10
monopole problem, 49–50

N

Newton, Isaac, 21, 29
nuclear fusion, 56–57, 59–60

O

observable horizon, 46–47, 68
orbitals, 13–15, 19
orbits, 21–23, 29

P

particle physics, 63–65
Penzias, Arno, 43–44
photons, 13–15, 19, 20, 56
photosphere, 18–19, 42
physicists, 7–8, 26–27, 46, 52–54, 63–64
prisms, 16–17, 19
protons, 13–15, 42, 63

Q

quantum gravity, 66
quantum mechanics, 27, 66
quasars, 57

R

radiation, 10–13, 42–44, 64
rainbows, 16–19
recessional velocity, 34
recombination, 43, 56–57
relativity, 28–30, 63, 66
Rubin, Vera, 23–24

79

S

satellites, 37–38, 40–42
scalar fields, 52–54
scientific notation, 52–53
scientists, 6–8, 18–19, 20–30, 31–34, 39–44, 52–54, 63–64
singularity, 9, 44
space-time, 28–30, 57–59
spectroscopy, 15–19, 33–34
speed of light, 26, 39
stars
   cepheid variable stars, 31
   formation of, 59–60
   speed of, 24
sun, spectrum of, 18–19
supersymmetry, 63, 65

T

telescopes, 37–38
temperature, 12–13, 40–42, 44, 52, 59
theories
   big bang, 8, 9, 44–45, 46, 50, 54, 55–59
   cosmic inflation, 8, 26–27, 34, 46–54, 56, 59, 66–68
   general relativity, 28–30, 63, 66
Type Ia supernovae, 27

U

universe
   beginning of, 8, 44–45, 46–47, 55–57, 68
   center of, 34–36, 72
   expansion of, 8, 26–27, 34, 46–54, 56, 59, 66–68
   future of, 57–61
   observable parts of, 39–45, 46–47, 68

V

vacuum energy, 26–27
vector fields, 51–52
velocity, recessional, 34

W

Wilson, Robert Woodrow, 43–44
WIMPs (weakly interacting massive particles), 63–65